Table of Contents

THE THEORY OF UNIVERSAL BALANCE IN HARMONY

World Economies and Environments in Balance

Steven Rhei Pena

Introduction

Have you ever wondered whether mankind and earth could live in balance and harmony together forever? Maybe you have or not or never really considered that the two go together. Well, the answer is yes, and the time is now to make sure we continue to co-exist without hurting one or the other! The evolution between mankind and earth has come together and are now at a crossroads! Mankind and earth are at a tipping point. If something is not done immediately and correctly, it could mean the end of mankind and earth as we know it today! What we do now is critical and will determine all existence of life, as well as the condition of earth. What we do now will make a huge impact, whether positive or negative, on all life for our future generations. Mankind is the biggest consumer of earth's resources. Earth has given us the resources for all life on earth, as we all know from either a scientific point of view and or religious one.

Earth has nourished and sustained all life for billions of years; its fruits nourish and sustains all life—including mankind—in the present, as they have done in the past. Balance and the usage of resources while rejuvenating the environment to a healthier state will be the key and the vital elements for mankind and earth to live together now and into the future in harmony. As of right now, one side of the equation—man—has for some time had the advantage over the other. The ideology or theory I present to you in this book offers a solution for both worlds to live together in balance and harmony—forever.

There are two parts to the theory, and both are essential for the solution to help mankind strive forward and learn to work along with earth with more care and consideration. It will take time, but in the long run it will be the right thing to do.

I have a question for you. What is very important to everyone on the planet, something that has no boundaries, prejudice, religion, values or morals, love or hate? Something that matters to rich and poor and affects every human being? The simple answer is money!

The first phase of this theory must be set in motion in order to start the second phase of the theory to bring about *Universal Balance in Harmony* into effect. The first part of this theory is an economic theory, outlining how to grow stronger and safer economies around the world without hurting the environment in the process. This system, once in place, will help to grow and should turn most or all economies around the world into a stable, cautious, environmental friendly, building innovation products, job growth boom for the greater good of mankind and earth.

I have another question for you to ponder. What is good for the earth and keeps everything under the blue sky safe and constant without changing the healthy state of earth while mankind multiplies and consumes everything, exhausting its natural resources? Complex answer, right? Every day earth is experiencing many variables, such as the state of the environment, natural resources, pollutants, the sun temperature, ultraviolet rays, air, space debris falling to earth, the orbital direction of earth, maybe a space storm or space bump in our path—all this, plus a whole lot more that we don't know. Still earth sustains the most precious thing on the planet—mankind, the biggest consumer of earth's resoures.

The best answer I have to this complex question is balance and constancy, meaning we all need to live in moderation, learning to safeguard and keep our earth at a constant healthy and natural state.

The second part of the theory starts once the economies around the world are thriving, like fine-tuning an engine so it runs steadily and smoothly. Once these economies around the world start running in the proper order for their own regions, then the second phase starts and *Universal Balance in Harmony* will be achieved.

After reading this book, everyone on the earth will have a better appreciation of their own nation or region, along with their natural resources and environment. We will look upon our regions—our homes—in a different light.

The strongest and healthiest economies should be the ones to lead by example. They should be the first to start to reverse the damage from years of environmental abuse and begin to heal earth. The nations of the world will democratically determine the most important issues to tackle first, as well as the safest and fastest methods to correct the issues. The United Nations will orchestrate this if all countries vote and agree. We need everyone to join around the world, with each nation around the world working in unity for the greater good for all life and earth starting in their own regions.

Balance Is the Key to Harmony!

Without balance, we all fail, and mankind and earth are doomed. If one or the other is off balance—too much or too little—then our home earth is at the hand of whatever invisible force—bad or good—that has the greater capacity to determine all our future mankind and earth. If balance is achieved through worldwide efforts in our environment, utilizing resources more efficiently—using more of what is good for our environment and less of what hurts our environment, then new ways of living will improve living environments and the well-being of earth, our home, and everyone and everything on this planet!

Then with our new lifestyle and new adjustments in our economies, **Balance will become New Harmony** and can save both mankind and earth to live and strive together forever.

For example, If we continue our fast way of living and creating new and more products without careful considerate considerations of impact they cause, we will be doomed sooner or later. We need to choose ways or methods of manufacturing and using products that will not damage the environment in the present and the future. We need to look at everything we do, from small to big; on land, underground, in the water, and in the air. If it's on or around our planet, we must understand its nature and where it fits with mankind and earth.

If we do not do this first step correctly, then someday soon mankind and earth will be doomed! If no change is made and we continue to consume without regard to the environment, then who do you think will suffer first, mankind or earth or both? Answer: both! We must slow down and think clearly and rationally about how much is too much. To what extent do we indulge ourselves at the expense of our environment—earth and all that lives on it?

Do we care about these things? If not before, then we should now. Scientists for decades have been warning us about many things that are wrong on our planet but has capitalism or commercial business really considered this heavy impact to the planet? Just in the last twenty to thirty years, some major businesses have started on the bottom of a mountain of environmental problems to fix. But it's not only for big business, but it is everyone's problem.

How about the lack of speed of intervention being done effectively from all governments contributing around the world? Do we want to take a chance to ruin our lives and world as we know it? The bigger nations are now starting to contribute with greater efforts now than any time before, but we still lagging big time.

We need every nation on the same sheet of music to really make an impact around the world to heal our earth to catch up to the past damage done already. Time is not on mankind's side; we need to move faster and smarter to save earth and ourselves. Is mankind around the world so ignorant and arrogant not to see the truth? Is man doing anything or enough today to make a difference for tomorrow? I do not think we are.

What is done today to remedy the problems will start to make a positive difference, which will help all of us around the world. "How important is this balance?" you ask. Let's say, hypothetically speaking, that the hole in our atmosphere, which we all know about from the news, journals, and scientific reports, is getting bigger each day and all those long ultraviolet rays keep pouring onto our earth faster and faster. They are being trapped here day after day because of the greenhouse effect caused by the pollution in our air from all sources—gasoline cars, factories, burning land, and other things around the world. This in effect starts a chain reaction so that the hole becomes so large that maybe our atmosphere starts to thin out faster than expected. Or may the air is broken up from its natural state and escapes into space; scientists can't figure out fast enough what to do or how governments can remedy the problem before it's too late!

As the earth is absorbing those intense ultraviolet heat rays and our earth heats up more each day, oceans rise, and plant and animal life starts to get sick and die all over the world. We wonder and ask ourselves "How?" and "Why?" How did we let this happen under our watch? Why did we let it get to this point?

I'm not a scientist, but just maybe, hypothetically speaking, this could happen. Maybe! But in reality some of these things are happening now. Also, our weather patterns are going out of normal sequence all around the world to some degree. Some say this is normal; others disagree. Either way, I don't want us to take a chance to see what might happen down the road.

So, better safe than sorry. I'd rather be on the safe side—fix it now and not wait. Food sources will become scarce as of lack of fresh water rain dries up streams and wells or droughts occur in areas that have never experienced drought before. This is happening now around the world.

These are some of the signs that, yes, something wrong is happening now and building up faster each day. The world's population is growing and has never been this big in history. This, too, is another hard element for earth to endure in the equation, as we used up fresh water around the world without replenishing, upsetting the balance between nature and mankind. There is a consequence to pay someday.

Failing to aid earth in keeping the balance is a recipe for disaster, for doom. To offset this loss of fresh water we should be making more smart water plants around the world to bring inline fresh water to keep a constant flow of fresh water in all areas needed for the survival. If we can make pipelines for oil, why not for the most precious element for mankind and life—water? As each day goes by with nothing being done to correct these problems all around the world, we are inviting disaster and doom for both mankind and earth.

Now, to remember this, how much do you value the air you breathe? I know you know this answer easy. Air is priceless to all living and not living things. Picture this as the days go by and you enjoy the simple things you take for granted each day—the joy of living, the joy of breathing. When the air becomes fouler each day with contaminants, which is happening right now in many regions of the world, people get sick and die. You might care or maybe not until it happens to you.

But what is even worse, I think we might start to lose our atmosphere and water source by vaporization to space. Will our air and oceans become dead and dry and vaporize into space? Most living things on earth will be all dead! This is a short version. I'm sure those with broader wisdom and understanding will understand in more depth the larger picture and process. But for now, this should get your attention.

This fine balance between mankind and earth is the main requirement to sustain our living with earth forever. If the economy keeps producing too many toxins to earth's air, land and sea, then our environment will change for the worse. Balance must be respected and not misunderstood. Mankind can or will perish forever! One more time I say to you, mankind can perish forever, like the dinosaurs and other species before.

After mankind is gone and earth is unbalanced, then earth will die, too, and become another desolate, bald lifeless planet in the solar system forever—no blue planet any more. Maybe our planet will look like Mars in the near future. So, to protect mankind and earth from this ever happening, we all must learn to compromise with every nation and work together all around the globe. We have to change our way of living every day for the better for balance and harmonious way of living with earth forever.

Earth has carried mankind for thousands or millions of years, and during this time, life was a struggle for mankind to overcome the elements. In the last two centuries, from the industrial revolution to the modern postindustrial revolution to services industries of today, the earth has grown more populated than any time in history. At the same time, it has run wild with its factories sprouting like mushrooms all over the world without consideration to earth and everything on it.

We are now at this moment, and we all know if we do nothing about what's happening to Mother Earth, it will not exist forever the way we know it today! Now is the time to stand up all around the world before we are too late. Stand together around the world as one brotherhood for mankind and say, "This will not be. I will not let this be!"

It's time for mankind to take control of the reins from earth to save ourselves and keep earth on the right track so life can flourish! Remember, we have already enjoyed the abundance of fresh air, land, food, water, seafood, byproducts, and every other type of material products that come from earth. Please do not take these elements for granted; they are the key to everything in existence here on earth.

We must all take responsibility for our actions, whether good or bad. All have a consequence. We must now set new, improved standards for ourselves and, most important, for earth. The future existence between mankind and earth depends on what mankind does now to fix past damages, utilize resources more efficiently, preserve and conserve today for the future for both worlds to co-exist in balance forever! Godspeed to all of us.

A Revolutionary Theory

This book will present a revolutionary theory, which is the main key and the very heart of the success for mankind and our world economies and earth to co-exist in balance and harmony. The two parts of the theory must work together so they fall into place smoothly, swiftly, and carefully to be most effective.

The economic part of the theory will help societies grow and reach their own safe full economic potential, creating a better, stronger, and safer status quo for their own economy. Those who embrace the theory with respect and employ it into their existing government structures will be the first to set in motion the *Universal Balance in Harmony Theory*.

Each nation around the world can have the comfort and peace in their minds and hearts when they start receiving the benefits of a thriving and growing economy, at the same time knowing the decisions that their government officials made or will make, will have an important enduring impact and careful considerations of safeguards for earth's utilization of finite resources, while protecting the earth's environment and healing earth in many different ways. All at the same time. This too, will offer a new way for governments—not just businesses—to have some control on earth's natural state of conditions to its environment and natural resources.

In the past, the demand for all goods was dictated by the demand of the people, the masses. This is not a good solution for Mother Earth or future generations. For example, we may consume seafood all around the world at the rate faster than we produce it because our consumption demand is too great and the main concern of business is profits, not Mother Earth or the preservation of natural resources. This lack of foresight is like the Roman Empire using up too many trees. Supply and demand unbalanced the scales, which led to the collapse of the empire. Without safeguards in place, capitalism is not a 100 percent safe way to run a society.

To remedy this problem, *Universal Balance in Harmony* will be the first and major check point that governments around the world can use to keep an eagle eye on all natural resources to keep them in safe balance. The scales need to be set on balance and stay that way as man and Mother Earth live together.

Every society needs to respect all natural resources, learn to better appreciate their resources, and to safely to grow at a steady rate without tipping the scales either way so mankind today and Mother Earth can live in peace and safety now and into the future.

For the first time, supply and demand won't dictate the availability of goods, but instead, government will determine the utilization of resources that should be best set in place to protect all of us. Governments should try to make the best decision for free enterprise and the law of supply and demand but with broader safeguards to protect earth and finite environmental resources.

Governments should develop new approaches to stimulate commerce in such a way that supplies will always be wisely used, with just enough for the present and leaving enough to conserve for future generations as well. All these safeguards and ideologies must be in the mixed into the equation each time a new innovation or product is introduced to the world.

Every world economy setting up this new theory into its own structure will help promote and protect the balance between mankind and earth to co-exist in balance in harmony forever. Working with this new foundational economic theory is the key element in helping to solve the problems of mankind and earth from the past, in the present, and into the future. Once in operation in governments around the world, this theory becomes our new foundation to carry forth all life and more efficient guidance over earth's resources now and into the future, and it must be respected by all who live on earth.

As a neutral organization that the world already knows, the United Nations (UN) should be the central base hub, if determined by a democratic vote of all nations. This main base headquarters will help all willing nations to improve the environment and economics in their regions and to help them understand their roles in the world. The UN will help establish which resources need to be conserved and which can be used freely as well how new methods can be used for the greater good of the countries and for the world. Each nation will have its ups and downs, give and take, but each must be willing to cooperate with goals that are reachable and attainable within a reasonable time frame.

All nations are welcome to join the *Universal Balance in Harmony* project, since we all live here on Mother Earth. Participation is voluntary, but it behooves every nation to participate. The project will benefit all humanity and national economies, and it protect the environment. Every nation has free choice, but the ultimate balance will come to earth when all nations participate and put this essential theory in operation. If most or all nations take part, we and future generations can enjoy earth now and forever.

Healing past wrongs to our environment—oceans, air, land, plants, animals, and rivers—will be a great step forward toward earth and mankind living in balance together forever.

The worst practices that cause the most damage to our resource are like cancer to earth. Once each nation learns how to eliminate those practices and use effective methods as well as to determine which problems they need to address first, then the healing will begin!

Using the *Universal Balance in Harmony* theory, countries will change their economies for the better in a way that allows them to prosper safely and conservatively in business and to use natural resources efficiently and respectfully. Then every nation around the world, whether their contributions are great or small, will be part of the global efforts to heal the world. One region at a time!

This mindset of nations working together in unity will bring more cooperation and help create stability, peace, and growth. It will bring a better awareness with broader understanding and respect to one another, building greater brotherhood and respect for one another in each region and the entire world.

This new method will broaden the perspectives and understanding of the public and governments from region to region, which will help policy makers to make policy changes that will meet the goals of the individual nation as well the world. Every nation is part of one great engine, and under this theory, all the parts work smoothly together.

This method will provide a more transparent view of governments to the world, which in turn will help build stability. Once a year, the United Nations should give a report card on every participating nation, its agendas, goals, and accomplishments.

In this first phase of the theory, new and better safeguards should be added to protect and keep economies flourishing while protecting earth at the same time. All who live on earth will want to be safe and will understand and appreciate the value of our home here. We all will live happier lives with more appreciation, knowing that all around the world, every nation is combining gallant efforts and that decisions were made with the best intentions for all who live here now and into the future.

Not only mankind, but also all other life depends on

the survival of mankind and earth coexisting in balance and harmony.

This theory, *Universal Balance in Harmony Theory*, should be the top priority for every nation on earth now because it sets the stage for new and humble beginnings for countries to work together with the objective to care for everyone and our planet earth. Nations will have different agendas, but the outcome, purpose, and goal is for the world to save Mother Earth.

This goal should blanket earth and everyone should feel part of this new fellowship, which should make all nations more concerned for their fellow nations. This type of care, love, respect, and understanding of one another will help stabilize and grow each region while simultaneously protecting the home of everyone on the planet!

Every economy has supply and demand, wants and needs. Each economy must daily face its consumption of resources for its own demanding and growing population. Until now, each country around the world has been working alone to meet the needs of its population and grow its economy. Because of the lack of world unity, most nations run their economies blindly without knowing the harm they are doing to their own environment or to the rest of the world.

Most nations are at fault, even the countries who are now trying to protect resources and to fix past wrongs. They are still not at full compliance with what really needs to be done now. But most countries are focused on their own populations' needs and wants, which keep on expanding. In these countries, there is little consideration of the harm to earth or the limits of finite resources.

Once these resources are gone, they're gone from Mother Earth for good! That region of natural resources is lost forever. We all must use our natural resources in moderation and more efficiently, cautiously, and wisely.

There must be a system of checks and balances in place to oversee natural resources. And I do mean everything—plants, soil composition, fresh and salt water, animals, air, insects, minerals, and more. Everything needs to be in balance so mankind and earth can coexist indefinitely.

Our process of burning up all our resources now without careful consideration of the consequences will leave us nothing for generations to come. That is how past civilizations made themselves extinct from the planet.

Wasting natural resources was one of many causes for the fall of the Roman Empire. The empire burned up too many trees to make more steel weapons to conquer new territories and to sustain their lifestyle, stretching the limits and boundaries that were impractical to grow. Once the empire exhausted the trees, it could not keep up with the growing demand of the Roman Empire, the new status quo. This lack of foresight in failing to replenish trees as they were used up serves as a good example of finite resources being used up too fast.

The ignorance of mankind along with today's selfishness—the ideology of greed, the constant desire for more—causes a repercussion from earth. The lack of resources (trees) created a major setback, one of many circumstances that brought down the Roman Empire and sent civilization into the Dark Ages.

Other strong civilizations, such as the Mayan, Aztec, Easter Island, and others, have all become ghost civilizations from similar experiences. These are examples of how important this fine balance of living along with all life and working with earth is!

As Al Gore said in his Nobel Peace Prize lecture "Our Purpose," the world has been getting out of tune for some time now. Mother Earth is dying slowly because of our abundant way of living and lack of care for the earth and life on it. Mankind has affected the planet and all life on it, from the ground to the air to the seas, as well as all who depend on nourishment from earth. Mankind has been like a silent parasite killing our own home slowly, and Mother Earth will someday turn on us. The time is now for our generation to understand the critical condition of the earth and to fix it before it is out of our reach and out of control.

This theory I present forth works for both mankind and earth. The two parts work together, like one stone knocking out two birds at one time. If you think this is impossible, think again; in my religion, all things are possible if you have faith in God. Yes, one man can make a difference.

Supermen and Politicians

We can see the power of what one man can do if we reflect on the many Supermen and heroic acts as well as motivation speeches throughout mankind's existence.

John F. Kennedy's words to the American people, well-known in the United States ring in my head: "Ask not what your country can do for you—ask what you can do for your country." Take out the words *your country* and put *earth* in their place, and you will understand the duty of all of us to do our part while we live a fulfilled life now.

Among the nations of the world today, there are approximately 7.4 billion people. In this mix of people, they are many individuals who are gifted in different ways. Some have a higher intelligence or wisdom in many different forms—smart innovators; geniuses; those with highly creative minds; people with emotional intelligence, systematic intelligence, compassionate intelligence, or a passion for understanding different outcomes; and more, a great mix of minds with different types of I.Q. These people who want to use their talents to make a difference and care for mankind will become known or are already known from sociological point of view as the Supermen Factor (S-Factor) people. These S-Factor people will help mankind live better lives as well as protect the environment and keep it healthy, safeguarding the fine balance of everything on our home—Earth.

These S-Factor people, who can be from any place or any walk of life, can help their own nations and the rest of the world to prosper and flourish with earth without hurting it.

Along with the S-factor people, we need better-rounded, righteous, smart policy-minded politicians who are compassionate, unselfish, and intelligent. These politicians must seek the best for the whole and not for themselves or a select few around the world. Leaders in each country's legislature or other governing body will make the decisions that make this theory work.

Governments around the world, including the government of my country—the United States of America, have all the tools to put this ideology into place quickly. Some other countries around the world might be as fast as the US, some faster, some slower. It all depends on how hard each government strives to perfect the system in its country.

The first phase—the economic phase—is designed to someday wipe out all national debt and all taxation. This won't happen overnight but as this theory or formula starts proceeding in our government system, then taxes will be gradually reduced and eventually eliminated at the same time the national debt is paid off.

This new approach will ease tensions of today's governments and societies and will fuel economies to grow while protecting earth from now on. Yes, you read correctly—this theory is designed to eliminate taxes and national debt, as well to sustain and grow any government while it equalizes the balance between mankind and earth's resources, safeguarding the environment—keeping it in balance while simultaneously healing previous damage to the region.

The condition of earth's resources will be much more transparent to the public in our country and around the world from now on. That means everything from the universe and sky to the core of the earth. This broad new approach and understanding will help us better understand ourselves. It will help us create new challenges and discover new innovative ways to perform or create things better, more efficiently, and in sync with protecting our most precious planet.

This theory, once implemented and functioning in a nation's economy, will show all nations around the world what is happening in a country or region with more transparency. Citizens in societies can have a better understanding of what's happening in their regions and in the world; they can see which resources are plentiful to utilize to create the next big innovation for themselves or world.

One thing I like too mention too that I learned in my studies while in college that in the beginning of America as towns where being built across America the USA now there used to be this big bird or pheasant that was almost as big as a turkey with a taste in between chicken or turkey or even better. People in that day lived in for survival mode and food did not come from a grocery store around the corner like it is in most countries today. These birds fly no more or will never be in existence again, all because of the ignorance of mankind in that generation.

You see, these birds were so plentiful at one time that when they flew over towns on their migration route, they would block out the sunshine in the sky as they travel. It would stay dark for some time, so people in those towns would stop what they were doing, grabbed their shotguns, run outside and shoot as many as they could each time. They had no consideration for the bird or pheasant because of their ignorant and self-indulging way of thinking at the time. It looked to them like there must be abundance of these birds everywhere.

Now, multiply that mentality by the number of towns they flew over during the 1800s, just about 100 years. As time went on, fewer and fewer birds flew over these towns, and people thought that the birds must have gotten smart and gone someplace else. But they were wrong. Without careful consideration, the people assumed they could never kill all those birds.

Have you ever heard of bird pie? No, of course not in our generation. But in the past here in America, it was a great dish to eat. If you watch some of the old cartoons, such as Heckel and Jeckel, from the mid twentieth century in the USA, you would see bird pies on the window ledge to cool off after baking. To make it known it was a bird pie, they would stamp the pie with bird feet markings or put the bird feet sticking out of the pie to make no confusion of what type of pie it was.

The last of these great birds known to be left in America died at some zoo in the early 1900s. How sad for the animal that its species is gone forever, and how sad that today we could have prevented this from happening. People around the world would have loved to eat this great bird, which might have been a great delicacy. What a loss to the present and future generations for mankind.

This is why I say in this book that we must learn more and understand better about everything—living and not. Find the safe point between too many and too few of anything so something can be done to keep the balance before either side gets out of hand.

Now, if balance is not maintained and one side of the equation gets off to the right or left—or worse, if we kill off another species or burn off another finite resources, we will see that one thing affects another somehow. Like one domino falling over on another, one thing will lead to another until we ourselves are affected in some way.

These problems, like the example above, must be fixed one by one all over the world. With a growing population worldwide, we must preserve what we have and curb our wants and needs so that we can sustain the earth. We must heal and protect our world with life and plants and an abundance of food and resources from any other harm, even from space.

Earth needs to get to as close to 100% or better of its efficient balance capacity between mankind and all natural resources, living and not. Problems with air quality, animals, land, nutrients and soil composition, oceans and their water temperature, lack of fresh water wells, underground streams and rivers need to be solved and fixed.

Every nation on earth should know its place better and do its own diligence to make their region a safer habitant to themselves and everything. And I mean *everything* around them, from the ground they walk on to the food they eat from their land, the air they breathe, and all natural resources and all byproducts man produces now. Each country needs to conserve for the future to produce a better quality of life with safeguards to protect earth and to fix past wounds to earth.

This new method should become the norm for the world. Once a year at its ceremonial annual meeting, the United Nations should recognize the achievements and accomplishments of each country and present awards for contributions to balancing and healing the world. Every nation who makes progress should be recognized by the United Nations. We all need pats on all our back to motivate us to success.

As each country fine tunes itself to perfect *Universal Balance in Harmony* in its government, balance will bring harmony to all life and earth. This won't happen overnight, but with time and perseverance, it can be done.

The implementation of the theory in any government will create a super boom for mankind—not just for one economy, but for economies all around the world—and will simultaneously create jobs and safeguard the balance to sustain all life on earth and beyond. This theory is designed to relieve the burden of ever-increasing taxes and, in fact, to eliminate them, while building economic growth in its society with more effective use of natural finite resources in moderation and putting safeguards in place to protect our environment.

I would like to see my country be the first to implement this theory. It already has in many ways, but now we need a broader spectrum with more focus on earth's balance of everything, living or not, and then with a growing economy. Once in motion, it will start to build revenue. It will not happen overnight, but with perseverance it will be done.

It will be a wonderful moment to see my own nation pay its national debt and turn into a surplus nation. I would love to see one day the national debt clock go backwards! I will be even more ecstatic with joy if every other nation on earth pays its debt and becomes a surplus nation—free from burden of debt for good and in balance in harmony with earth. What a relief to nations all around the world. What a joy!

It is so powerful that its implementation will put mankind back into the space race to advance our civilizations to other planets in our solar system and beyond to other universes and galaxies. The theory will help strengthen and promote future space endeavors to harness the resources in space for the vitality to our existence and expand mankind to live among the stars all over the universe and beyond.

Earth should always be preserved from harm and damage so it will be a permanent home to mankind forever. Let's all heal and keep earth safe to all life and natural resources in balance forever!

Mankind must seek and find resources other than earth to sustain itself so that mankind and earth can stay in balance forever. Space, the final frontier, should be our new conquest for mankind's expansion for living and to find more resources. Scientists and politicians working together should be more transparent to one another and to the public and make the best choices to speed the economic process and protect the environment and finite resources. This theory, which promotes economic growth in new ways while simultaneously healing Mother Earth, will be and is the key to balance and harmony so that all humanity and future generations can live in the present and happily ever after.

Theory 101 Introduction

Implementation of the theory begins with an injection into society of new innovations. Businesses producing earth-friendly products or services will be donated for some time for a given fee by S-Factor citizens to the government. The revenue from these businesses will stimulate the economy along with safeguarding resources while reversing harm done in the past in order to promote *Universal Balance in Harmony*. A general explanation of how the theory should work follows.

Economic Theory
for Mankind

The United States of America consists of fifty states and districts and territories that are not yet states. Each state and district contains people, including entrepreneurs and innovators. I'm sure that most people enjoy sports, whether watching or participating. This competitive mentality will provide the impetus to manage our economy and earth to help promote *Universal Balance in Harmony* for generations to come.

We will learn to compete in each state, region, or district for the best inventions—the best products, methods, and services, whichever are the best choices at the time for earth first than mankind. The very best innovations from each state, district, or region best suited for the economy and friendly to the earth will be selected by the elected officials from the state, district, or region. The innovations that are selected at the local levels then move to House of Representatives (here in the USA) to further narrow down the selections. Then the Senate and the President do the final analysis and selection.

The new method set forth below offers a new kind of

thinking and processing for our government to introduce and process bills and appropriations in a more business-like fashion to serve the nation. We would need to reform and fine-tune parts of our government for this ideology to work effectively. We might even have to add some new amendments to our Constitution for the greater good for our nation, humanity, and earth. Godspeed to all!

Without further ado, I present to you the **"Universal Balance in Harmony"** operational system theory as it could work in the United States and in all nations around the world.

My country has a population of approximately 319 million people in our fifty states and other districts. As described above in the discussion of S-Factor people, we have many educated people. In this mix we have many innovators with brightly creative minds and with all different types of intelligence—minds who can make a difference in our country and earth.

Our government already gives out grants for new innovations but now things will work differently. The government itself will help decide which innovations or services should be put out through a selection process for the best innovations for the environment and the economy.

Most innovators, even if they have a grant from the government, still do not have enough working capital to start a company, create the infrastructure for their venture, or maintain it once it gets off the ground. They look for help from banks, family members, and friends. Often the innovators do not obtain sufficient funds to grow or advance their innovative ideology or new invention to the world. Bringing an invention to fruition takes a lot of money and a lot of time.

Independent small innovators usually do not have either of these, so they need aid from others, which usually proves difficult, as does trying to succeed alone. This dilemma has been going on for ages.

As time moves forward, these innovators die, and a lot of new innovations or services or inventions go to the grave. These new inventions and ideas could have provided mankind a better way of life in many different ways, and humanity suffers when the innovations and inventions aren't developed. A tragedy of wasted talent and effort! Gone for good! What a shame. Discouraging when you really think about it. How many are in the graves now?

If only these failures could be avoided. Just think how beneficial these innovations could have been for humanity and society. How more advanced our society could have become. The opportunity cost of new jobs that didn't get created. The ripple effect of more new jobs created from just this one great innovation can impact society from lost growth or lost (GDP) gross domestic products or services in an economy that never materializes.

The world, state, region, and federal government all lose out on the possible additional revenues these new ventures would have generated in taxes (now). If only some of these striving enterprises had ever taken off the ground. But these innovations died!

This new theory will change all this. We will no longer

lose these innovations and miss out on experiencing the economic benefits that could have come from had those failures succeeded. From now on, we will eliminate this sort of problem once and for all.

The concept of taxes has been around a long time. The system has been good and bad to all of us in some ways, but it's now time for change! I want to stress that taxation was a good idea to help societies grow. It was a great innovation that benefited man, but all things come to an end or are modified for the better. Taxation is an old method to create wealth for governments.

It's time for a new ideology that will allow governments to do their job without shortfalls in funds and going into debt. This will strengthen our country and any country, which, in turn, will help improve their citizen's well-being, balance environments, and heal earth in the process in their regions.

This new ideology will fuel job growth and provide stability for mankind to keep multiplying—without taxation and without hurting earth. This laissez faire ideology should be addressed and understood for a better fit with our way of life and the ways of life of societies around the world. Laissez faire is an economic doctrine that rejects government interference in commerce beyond the minimum necessary for the free enterprise system to operate following its own economic law.

This doctrine should do for the economy what our forefathers intended it to do from the beginning, but it should be reformed for government to intervene when necessary to protect and balance the environment.

Our government will now be involved in the process to help create new innovative businesses to build its own economy and create safer conditions for mankind and earth to coexist in balance and harmony. If current laws do not permit this, then we must change the law or add a Constitutional amendment so that the *Universal Balance in Harmony* theory can take root and grow. Under this theory, our government will grow in a positive direction for the economy that works in the interest of the citizens in the nation as well as the citizens of the world and that protects and balances the environments.

All nations around the world should work together to bring earth to 100 percent or better living capacity for all things, alive or not. By things *not alive* I mean like oil, natural gas, minerals, and things in that nature. If we exhaust all the oil on earth in the next 100 to 500 years, what will future generations have to sustain themselves? Oil byproducts will always be part of our life and for future of mankind for a long time.

Now is the time for our generation to take action to safeguard resources and no time to waste. This generation must start fixing the problem now before it turns out to be that bird that disappeared on us of because of the lack of foresight now or overindulgence on goods we receive now.

We need to consider now and into the future that we all can enjoy living modestly in every generation. Even better, we can use other energy sources that are effective to meet Mankind's wants and needs and also at the same time to heal Mother Earth and keep her healthy.

Revenue

Revenue pays the bills and helps governments run smoothly. It comes mainly from local taxes, state taxes, and federal income and other taxes. Citizens of each country have paid taxes to support their governments, so that governments can help their citizens through infrastructure and endowment programs.

Imagine that the government was run like a business, and its main job was to ensure that the earth, its nation, and its citizens got the attention first. The focus would always be on earth first, then mankind.

The federal government would work with the states, and the states would work with local municipalities all the way down to the people. That happens now, except under the new system, the government would not look for tax monies from any of these departments anymore. Instead, it will be looking for the next very best ideas, innovations, services, or inventions that will best fit the commerce in their economies while benefiting the environment.

The government will establish businesses to produce and market the innovations. Once in operation and moving forward, the new businesses will create stability and job growth. At the same time, they will produce positive revenue, fueling and sustaining the government and growth of the nation's economy. *Universal Balance in Harmony* at work here will become the new norm to generate revenue for the government.

Under *Universal Balance in Harmony*, the government will buy and borrow first from willing volunteers, whom we will call the Supermen or Superwomen, the S-Factor citizens. These creative innovators and inventors will give up the rights to their inventions/innovations/ideas for a specific period of time and will be compensated by the government for the rights that will be used to generate government revenue. The government will make and sell the new products or services to produce positive revenue and will compensate the S-Factor citizens for the rights they give up.

This system will both help maintain the status quo of our government with its existing programs and also instigate growth in our national economy. It will also create jobs, new innovative jobs in a safe haven for the earth, and produce new employment growth in diverse directions in the states or districts in which they originated.

Then after the allotted number of years (ten to fifteen) pass, the government can sell this venture to the inventor at a depreciated cost. If the inventor does not want to buy the business, then the government of the inventor's home state has the second option to buy from the federal government and owner. If the state does not want to buy the company, then the federal government can keep running it at a buyout price from the State and inventor.

The government can keep the business or sell it to the

highest acceptable bidder in the nation or anywhere around the world. The new buyer must intend to operate the business in a safe locality in a state or country that is the best fit in safeguarding balance in natural resources for the best interest of earth first, then mankind!

This approach is voluntary and does not interfere with other free commerce and capitalist businesses, unless a venture creates a high risk to earth and humanity going out of balance. At that time, new laws must be set up to protect the environment and resources to stay constant and in balance.

The inventor's home state as well as the federal government would receive an agreed-upon percentage of the income from each business. The exact percentages can be worked out when the theory is structured into the government process.

The goal of this theory is to preserve humanity, provide stability and growth, and use finite resources in moderation, in an intelligent, safe, and conservative fashion to keep earth from going out of balance. We need to reverse previous damage to bring earth to 100% or better of its capacity to improve abundance to all life—air, water, and land.

This calls for the best conservation and preservation methods, which will be used all around the world—first starting in our own region. Preservation methods will be used everywhere on our lands and lakes to reproduce healthier fish, animals, and plants, as well as better composition of the soil to avoid any extreme conditions that would offset the balance for life for mankind and earth. Balance must be respected and is the main key to sustain all life as mankind's population grows into the future!

Mankind must learn to live closely together with all life on earth. One objective of this two-part theory is to help mankind avoid completely exhausting earth's resources and using them unwisely and too quickly, with no regard to the environment.

This theory is intended to help governments around the world improve economic growth in their societies without damaging their regions and earth. All countries around the world should come to a consensus and use this theory wisely so that we eliminate some of the most serious problems earth presents today and at the same time our economy.

The first step is for all governments around the world to put *Universal Balance in Harmony* theory into motion. This will create a super boom of job growth or a steady job growth into the future yet to be seen.

While we build our economies, we all will strive to eliminate national debt and reduce taxes. Implementation of the theory will require hard work and dedication with wisdom, patience, and understanding. If efforts are successful, we will keep constant population growth in check with the right amount of balance for mankind's wants and needs and earth's ability to provide them now and into the future.

Once these new innovations or methods businesses that are earth friendly are in place and striving for the better good for mankind and earth, then I would like to see changes take place in my own country. The United States will be able to gradually reduce taxes and pay the national debt and over time will eliminate taxes for good—a dream come true for many!

Societies were built by taxing citizens, who pay the government to build their civilizations. Although a burden to citizens at times, taxes help advance society to higher standards. This theory that allows the government to own and operate innovative businesses provides the same benefits as taxes, but with the citizens in mind to share and work along with government. These new innovations will improve our way of life and enable us to live more effectively and wisely.

This theory is designed for citizens to help citizens and for the right chosen people in policy positions in government to have the power to say nay or yea. The S-factor citizens innovating and working along with government officials will aid and help in the process to choose the best solutions that are best for both mankind and Mother Earth in their regions and the world. Societies will be lifted in many ways: getting out of debt; creating more jobs; getting out of a stagnant economy; and creating a safer, stronger, growing economy while simultaneously balancing, safeguarding, and healing the earth.

Maybe most job growth will come from new methods and services designed to heal the earth as fast as possible!

As this economic first phase of this theory is striving forward then I would like to see certain factors take place to keep their status quo in check and help improve stability around the world. Again I say, first goal , pay off the national debt and bring it out of indebtedness and then bring it to a surplus nation of funds, which in turn strengthening secures and stabilize its own currency. Second, then the government could reduce taxes until they are totally eliminated. Third, to use the revenue from the S-factor innovation businesses, to fuel all government programs and build new ones if need be. This new type of income injecting into the government would help pay the national federal budget each fiscal cycle, sustaining and expanding all federal programs—Social Security, Medicaid, Medicare, the Military, and others-along with infrastructure across the nation. The system will encourage an infinite number of new programs, all in sequence so the country can maintain its status quo with room to grow positively with earth in mind forever.

It will be a great relief for one's own country and for the world to grow in stability. It will be the opposite someday than the way it is now. We hear so much negativity from the news about countries on the brink of going bankrupt—inflation, hyperinflation in some countries, currency collapsing in a nation, clashes, riots, shortages of foods and goods and services, and lack of medical care due to indebtedness, without any way to sustain itself for the present or into the future to help to build itself in such a way to get out of debts. The only relief is the IMF or better known to the world, the International Monetary Fund. They regulate currency values to each and every nation on the planet whom are members. They are the ones to devalue or increase a currency value and help any nations who need to borrow or help to sustain their economy. They help poor nation's infrastructure: roads, water wells, schools, things like this to build a society. It is there for all nations to work together for the greater good for themselves and earth.

This theory will shed a beam a light to my country as well as the world of relief so all nations can focus on what your particular nation needs to do to get on track to know your place in the grand scheme in this world. This way all can contribute to their own economy the right way and help themselves and the world out of the dark and into the light for all the world to, sustain, strive and heal—together. I'm excited for the world and for my own country.

Balance must be sustained with additional resources to protect the uncertainties that might rise into the future unchecked. For example, when you go on a camping trip, you make sure you have all the provisions to sustain yourself out on the field. You also prepare for whatever else you think might happen on your trip. In the same way, we have to ensure we have the resources we need now and are prepared for any contingencies that may arise in the future.

At times we may have to level off our standard of living to keep things balanced and to maintain the broader picture for the benefit of everyone all around the world.

As a hypothetical example, if were consuming too much fish at a rate that endangers the fish itself or other sea life, a giant red flag would go up. We should never get to that stage, but if we do, we need to take drastic measures worldwide. That might mean that eating fish would be prohibited for a year or longer in order for the fish to grow and repopulate at a safe healthy level. The scientists or the

S-Factor people will know when it safe to start catching and consuming fish again.

We all are to blame for situations like this. From this point forward, there must be tighter control worldwide to keep the oceans safe so the world population can eat today and continue into the future at a safe, moderate pace.

We all must make sacrifices to make things right all around the world. If we forecast a lack of natural mineral resources to sustain mankind on Mother Earth for future growth, then we must go out from our normal boundaries and explore the final frontier of space to seek these natural resources.

Citizens of each nation can learn to compete among themselves in a friendly, voluntary way in their communities to help evolve their countries to a higher standard. Individuals with creative solutions and innovations for their own country and government will strive to achieve earth-friendly job growth as well as protecting the environment to bring stability and balance with harmony.

Innovation and Competition

I will use my country as a model for the rest of the world to better understand this concept. Competition among citizens in each of the fifty states will help propel mankind forward with job growth faster than the norm. The process breaks down citizen versus citizen, state versus state, or region versus region, depending on the area and the government in each country.

Every year, each state will ask its citizens to challenge themselves to bring forth better inventions, innovations that will help expand the state's or region's economic growth and safeguard the environment and earth. The inventions determined to be the best will be chosen for the government to build businesses to produce the product or service. The positive cash flow of the businesses will provide jobs in the local area and will bring revenue to that region, state, and the federal government.

As this process is multiplied year after year, our economy will grow faster and safer than ever before. This new method of placing these new innovations around the nation may even create a super boom with checks and balances for earth.

Each state's goal is to come up with many innovations, then select the top twenty-five from the state to present to the federal government. The competition would also be conducted in US territories like Puerto Rico, Guam, and American Samoa.

Scientists and experts from various fields, along with the inventors, will work to aid in this process to help legislators in the House of Representatives and Senate have broader understanding of the impact of the innovations selected from each State. The ideas will be fine-tune to ensure they benefit the environment and then society. They will be presented to legislators, and the top innovations selected in the House will sent for a vote by the Senate.

The Senate determines its choices for the best innovations, explains the reasons for their choices, and submits its recommendations to the President of the United States to veto or pass.

This will create a new method of running our government for the good of our citizens, world, and earth!

The House of Representatives will be making selections from 1250-plus submissions. That is based on twenty-five state winners from each of the fifty states plus submissions from US territories. The sole job of the Legislators and President is to select the ideas that are offer the most long-term benefits for earth first and the wants and needs of mankind second.

These innovations will have different degrees of importance and originality, ranging from totally new to new modifications on old inventions. The newest will usually take precedence over modifications to older innovations. However the decisions will be made by the legislators and S-Factor citizens. The Congress along with the President will select as many innovations as the country can afford.

Within the House of Representatives and Senate, legislators will select and work with top specialists—scientists and other experts—to aid them in their deliberations. These people joining in the ranks with the legislators will not be Republicans or Democrats or members of any other party. A good name that is fitting for the USA. would be *Ultra Patriots*. The Ultra Patriots—inventors, scientists, experts, and legislators—would work together as one team with one goal.

I don't want to go off on a tangent directly here about any or all political parties, but enough is enough of losing sight of solutions and goals for the nation, the people, and earth. It's not about parties and never has been; it's about our nation, our people, who we live together with—our fellow brothers and sisters here and around the world. It's about humanity, about mankind and now—so important—earth!

It's not about bragging rights about which a better party is or which party produces the most Presidents or how members feel when their party is really the best when in control of the Senate. This nonsense with an ego for one's party does not do any good for the citizens of the country. At times I feel they just looking for producing the next President and getting credit and brownie points for their party from the American public.

This main two-party (and sometimes more) system only divides us. One party while in control in the Senate and White House helps one side of the country for a term of years, but then the other side suffers during that time. Then the other party wins the next race and the opposite side suffers for another term of years. In this party chess game, each term and cycle the American people see and know the outcome. Finger pointing, deliberation, saying, "No it's your fault."

It's a vicious cycle; it's old and I hear a lot from folks who say the system is broken. This cycle does not benefit the country as a whole, whether the President is a Democrat or a Republican. This way of running our government has been bringing down the whole country. Why, for what or who? For personal bragging rights from each parties? It goes on and on to where?

Hate, fear, bragging rights, jealousy, and playing the game of who's better are not good traits to have in leadership roles in any country, especially under God anywhere and particularly in high levels of government!

I see it many times when Republicans and Democrats can't come to a consensus. I would prefer that legislators were judged only how they voted that day or that year. People today our more educated than any time in our history. We see, we understand, we care.

Instead of working together for the greater good for the masses and reaching compromise solutions for the whole country, parties play politics like a ping pong ball, focusing on which party is going to get the credit from the American people! It's a waste of the American tax dollars to see them act this way.

The real losses—time, good effort, money, and opportunity costs—occur to our nation's citizens, our economy, and our environment. There is no time anymore for us to live this way. There are bigger and more important issues in the country and world now.

Rather than favoring their particular special interests groups and investors who have more money and time, politicians should help all sides as well, mainly the masses. The new politicians' thinking should focus on the environment, people, and the state of the nation.

Our government could have changed long ago but those who could make the change haven't really figured how to, but this book should enlighten everyone. This new theory will help eliminate that old style of thinking and will bring a whole new way of getting things done. It will provide more transparency from our governmental leaders. There will be no more parties pointing the finger at each other. Now all parties will be accountable as one and working for the benefit of the earth and its people. Each politician should have a broad intellectual understanding and a strong empathy and a stronger dedication for earth and mankind.

Now, to get back to business. The inventors will give up their rights and complete ownership to their innovations to the government in his or her country. The government of the nation will build that innovation product or services into a business, hire employees, and manufacture and market the product or service for a minimum of ten to fifteen years.

The federal government, along with the state, will have total control of the innovation and, if necessary, any additional input from the inventor as needed and agreed. A higher percentage of the gross profit will go to the federal government first, then a smaller percentage will go to the state, and a smaller percentage will go down to local municipalities where the government business sets up. The specific percentages will be worked out and agreed upon by all the parties—federal government, state, local municipalities, and inventors.

The inventors will be rewarded a fairly sum for their opportunity cost lost, which is negotiable, for the rights to their inventions or innovation. For example, the federal government might pay each inventor at least a million dollars per year for the first five years in business. Then beginning in the sixth year, the reward could be doubled or a different amount negotiated between Congress and the inventors, subject to the President'sfinal approval.

Each new factory or business in operation should be earth friendly, and information substantiating this should be publicly available. This new transparency will aid the entire world and help people understand better what resources will be used to produce the new innovations and where the resources will be taken from, depending on the scarcity or abundance in all regions of the world.

The S-Factor people will be the ones responsible along with political figures for improving the world in the present and into the future. This in turn will help all humanity strive for a new way of living and will even bring out healthier, higher, and safer living standards.

I say again, I recommend the United Nations to give an annual report to the world on *Universal Balance in Harmony* so everyone knows what's been done and what still needs to be done for the greater protection of mankind and the earth. If earth is in its best state of health or close to a safe health, then this will create better balance between earth and mankind. We need to stay in the safe zone where mankind and earth can flourish.

If the earth is sick and continues in a downward fall, then we will all suffer to the end and die before it earth dies. We need to put our efforts together and find the best solution that will enlighten us to when in history earth was in its prime or glory days. Our new goal will be to return to that glory point for earth's conditions to sustain life abundantly as the population worldwide increases. We need to bring the earth to a capacity to supply everyone's needs without hurting the environment, animals, plants, air, or water in the process. This is what I mean by *Universal Balance in Harmony*. Find the acceptable rate of growth and fine tune the balance.

We are running behind, and here's an example: Instead of having too many fish from our oceans, we are eating too much and faster than what the oceans can maintain. The balance is off; mankind is depleting the fish too fast, not giving them enough time to grow or produce in the wild fast enough.

Other factors like global warming might contribute to the problem. Even not developing enough fish farms worldwide to keep up with the demand for consumption is an issue. If we eat all the fish in our generation, then what will future generation eat from the oceans? Dead algae?

This is the balance I'm speaking about—for everything on the planet, living or not. There cannot be lack of foresight on all these problems.

This theory is a basic guide that should set the foundation of how our government will work more transparently to the public and world! If the innovation, product, service, or new method is successful, the government can hold on to the business for ten to fifteen years, but if it's not successful, the government can resign at any time. If the federal government resigns it, it will offer the company back first to the inventor at a depreciated price. If the inventor does not want it, then the state that put forth money in the beginning has the second choice to keep it for however many years are agreed between the government and the inventor. The state then pays buyout fees to the federal government and the owner or inventors. At this point, roles will be changing; instead of the federal government getting most the revenue, it will be the state's turn.

When this happens, money will funnel a new way now, the largest percentage of the profit will be going to the state, then some to the federal government, and a percentage of profit or fixed amount to the inventor.

If neither the state nor the inventor wants it, then the federal government has the third choice to buy the business outright from the state and inventor at a fair depreciated value. After the federal government owns the business in full, it can auction the venture off to any state or region within the country or to another country where it is best suited for the interests of the earth first and humanity second.

The government (US or any other) never owes penalties to itself, states or regions, or inventors if it buys the business.

The inventor's home state benefits with the US government in a share of the profits in an agreed-upon amount. The state may or may not contribute money depending on many variables, such as if the state is a welfare state, doesn't have enough funds to contribute, or has a lack of infrastructure and resources to create such an innovation.

The region could be a group of several states, which, along with the federal government, could contribute an agreed-upon amount of monies to help create to infra-structure, the facilities, to manufacture the new products or services.

The state or region will reap a twenty percent maximum return on net profit, with the remaining eighty percent of net profit going to the US government. Here are a few scenarios can better explain how the process will work.

State And/Or Region Maximum Return Along With US Government

Innovation (Alpha) costs 100 million dollars for the infrastructure to manufacture the invention.

US government puts down 80% of the total	$80 million
State or region puts down 20% of the total	$20 million
Total	$100 million

This is the final cost to create the new business: $100 Million.

The US government after expense will receive 80% maximum return on all net profit for the next ten years to fifteen years.

The State will receive from the US government a 20% return on net profit for the next fifteen years, depending on the circumstances involved. The norm will be ten years because usually after ten years the innovation is on a down-turn of its product life cycle.

The percentage to the state government might have to be adjusted up to 30% or 40%, depending on how much expenditures the US government and the state or region actually needs and can afford at that time.

The innovator will receive one to two million dollars or a percentage of the profit agreed upon between the government and the inventor for the first five years. The amount would be doubled or increased by another agreed-upon amount for years six to ten or fifteen.

After seven years, the exclusive patent and design rights are forfeited, and the product can compete in the free market. However, anything can be modified based on the situation, the wants and needs of the business, and, most important, the welfare of earth. We will cross that bridge at that time.

This is an example on how this can work, but the parties can negotiate an agreement that is most advantageous to all concerned.

Final approval will come from the consensus vote from all Ultra Patriots (ALL PARTIES) and Congress with Presidential approval.

The best approach in keeping this method or ideology moving forward is to always keep it simple and fair. Most important, we must make sure that all newly created innovations are in the best interest of the earth—to balance and heal the environment.

State and/or Region Minimum Return along with the US Government

Innovation (Alpha) costs 100 million dollars for the infrastructure to manufacture the invention.

US government puts down 95% of the total	$95 million
State or region puts down 5% of the total	$5 million
Total	$100 million

The United States government will receive a 95% return on net profit.

The state will receive from the US government no less than 5% return on net profit for the next ten to fifteen years.

The inventor will receive one to two million per year or a small percentage that was agreed on with government. Compensation in years 1 to 5 will be a set amount and in years 6 to15 will be at least double the original amount.

Again, this is an example on how it can work, but it's not set in stone!

In both of these scenarios, the state is the middleman and contributes to the creation of the manufacturing business. Therefore, the state should have the main right to choose where the factory is built. If feasible, a larger percentage of local people should be hired to run the new operation, but this will be determined on a case-by-case basis. The US government will work with the state in its decision-making process to determine the best place to build the manufacturing plant.

If Opportunity Cost Is Lost

The federal government may determine that the invention should be produced someplace other than the state or region of the origin of the idea, depending on the availability of natural resources and the short- and long-term environmental balance. In this case, the US government must pay the state or region for the opportunity costs the state loses when the business is moved to another state or region or country.

This would be an extra 20% on top of the minimum (5%) or maximum (20%), for a new total of 25% minimum or 40% maximum. This will make it as fair as possible to the state and region, offsetting and compensating for loss of opportunity, cost of employment, and additional revenue in the state for its citizens.

After ten to fifteen years, the federal government's rights to run the business expire. The government can do two things: keep the business or sell it. If the government decides to sell, the creator/innovator has the first option to buy the business at a discounted/depreciated price.

The second option belongs to the state government. If the inventor doesn't want to buy the business at a depreciated price, after a payout to the original innovator, the state that originally invested in the venture can buy it from the government at a discounted price.

If the state does not want to buy it, the federal government will determine what to do with the company after paying the state and inventor their final payment. After that, the government can do as it wishes.

It could move the business to another state, region, or country. It could sell the company abroad to the highest bidder, as long as the location would be beneficial to the environment. State, regions, or countries whose environments fit the ideal profile for that type of business or services could be invited to bid at a special auction by the government.

If Inventor Keeps the Business

If the inventor/innovator decides to buy the business and keep it running, then the cash flow would go in a reverse fashion so that most the revenue would go to the owner/business/corporation. The federal government and the state would get some money back in a small percentage as long as the business is running and is profitable. The percentage of profit would be agreed between all parties.

If the owner decides to buy the business but wants to sell the venture for additional profit to the highest bidder worldwide, he can only do so with the approval and at the discretion of the government. The state would always have the first choice before any outside auction takes place. Only if the state does not want to purchase the business venture could it be sold to other states or regions. Other countries could buy the company only if no state want it.

The US government would have the final choice to buy out the individual or corporation. If the federal government does not want to buy the business back, the owner, with the guidance of the government, can auction it off to any country that is well-suited for the good of the earth first and humanity second.

The contract between the United States government and the inventor allowing Congress to auction off the venture to the highest bidder to any region on earth. The first choice is to the country of origin; the second to any other country in regions well-suited for this invention or services process.

In an auction, if the states or regions are selected first because of qualifications, then only the top three of the best candidate states or regions will be invited to attend the federal auction. If all the states failed to pass Congress's thoughtful criteria regarding the economy and earth's resources, countries that meet critical criteria for earth as designated by the United Nations will be selected by Congress to bid in the auction.

Maybe the United Nations should do the auctions for auctions abroad. These countries chosen to bid will be those best suited to benefit earth first, then mankind's wants and needs second. Congress, along with the President (or the United Nations if it conducts international auctions) will invite as many nations as meet those critical qualifications. The country making the highest bid wins the venture and all patents associated with it.

STATE BUY OUT OR WIN OVER

If the state buys the company from inventor, it must pay back to the United States government what it put into the venture at the beginning, but at a fair depreciated rate.

Example:

The United States government put forth in the beginning eighty million dollars out of the 100 million.

Since the market has leveled off within the ten to fifteen years, the depreciated of Alpha A would be approximately 10% of that value in ten years, about $8 million or a fair amount worked out between the State and United States government and innovator.

INVENTOR BUY OUT OR WIN OVER

If the owner or inventor or corporation decides to keep the business, it can make new changes with good consideration from the state or federal government or both to keep the present workers or even hire new ones. The inventor can fire at will without prejudice while downsizing if need to be, but he or she should try to keep a well-rounded and experienced staff from the time of federal and state ownership. The company belongs to the inventor now—he or she has already shared the wealth with the government, society, and the world. Now in return he or she gets to enjoy the fruits of his or her thoughtful labor—to run the business as he or she chooses.

The owner/inventor or corporation then pays back the state or region and United States government a small percentage of the initial investment with a depreciating factor for those ten to fifteen years.

Depreciated Buyout by Innovator from the Federal and State Governments

Since the market has probably been saturated in the last ten to fifteen years, the payback should be no more than 5%.

Example:

	Investment	**Payback %**	**Payback**
The US Government's initial cost	$80 million	X .05 (5%)	$4 million
The state's initial cost	$20 million		$1 million
Investment total and percentage payout	$100 million	X .05 (5%)	$5 million

The owner or inventor or corporation can pay back the US government and state whatever amount is agreed on for ten to fifteen years with no interest in a payment plan, or he or she can payoff in full to the State and US govvernment in one lump sum at a reduced amount as all agree.

United States Government Buy Out or Win Over

In this scenario, the United States government buys out the owner, inventor, corporation, or the state. The business then officially belongs to the US government, which can do whatever it wishes with it. It can keep the business where it is, relocate it to another state or region, or even send it overseas—whichever is best for earth and then mankind.

Depending on conditions of transfer or sale of the venture, the United States can be a main or light sponsor of this venture for the new host state, region, or country. The new host region or nation will work alongside the founding government or, depending on variable factors, the relocation of the venture might become efficient and self-sustaining over the short or long term. Such enterprise should be placed in an area with a demographic of qualified locals and experienced veterans from the company.

Each venture buyout will be different, based on the circumstances of earth and mankind's conditions and needs at that particular time. The government who original owns it will have the majority of power on the venture until the new host is capable of running the operation properly. This all, of course, depends on situations and conditions in transferring the buyout contract to a new buyer or new host state, region, or country. United Nations should be in charge to monitor and witness such agreements at auctions around the world; the UN would also be a mediator to handle any revisions or disputes and after negotiations and contracts are signed.

The Wheel: Universal Balance in Harmony Theory

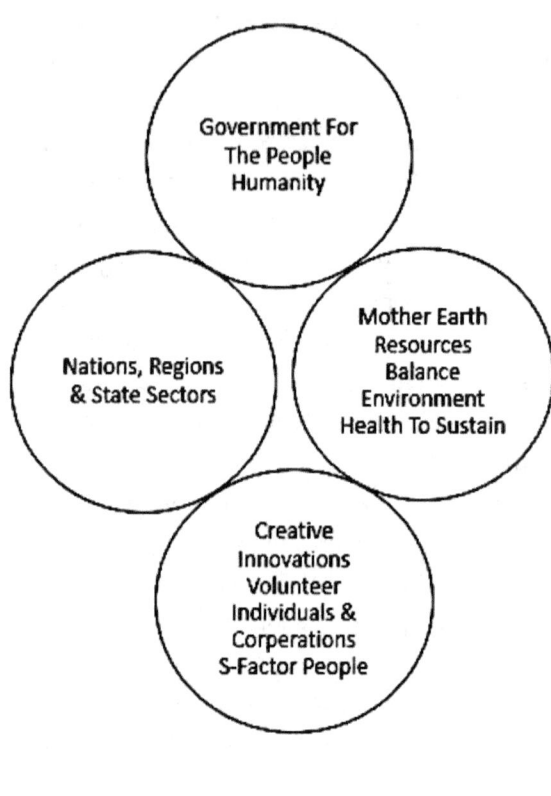

Figure 1

Circle of Universal Balance in Harmony

This new theory will spark and carry our country's economy or any government's economy and will have safeguard mechanisms to protect and balance everything living and not living on earth. This theory in short can be call an injection, a healing shot in the arm, for both earth and mankind to sustain and grow in balance with each other without destroying the other.

This ideology, if put in place by governments around the world, will strengthen mankind's alliances and governments as they co-exist with earth in balance and harmony. The diagram on this page is a "Universal Balance and Harmony" theory wheel cycle diagram. It shows the key to how we can help ourselves towards sustaining and growing our economy at the same time protecting precious resources, using them sparingly and wisely. The result will be the balance of the environment, allowing people to take advantage of other conservation and preservation methods to extend and preserve earth's resources to sustain mankind now and for generations to come.

This ideology will help all countries fine-tune or micro-tune their own governments in many different ways of evolving into a *Universal Balance in Harmony Theory* economy. At the same time, the governments will give consideration to what, how much, and where to use its natural resources to protect and heal earth. All nations will need help from one another some time or another. Help from other countries will unite us and strengthen our relationships with one another.

Our big brother, the "watch keeper" or United Nations,

will help and aid and guide us to success in our regions. This ideology will be the safety net that helps each section or region around the world improve and make known to themselves and the world how important every person and every place on earth is. Our careful vigilance to living well now while preserving and protecting vital resources and healing earth to the natural good healthy state it once was—or even better, will keep things in balance. This will give future generations the joy of life that we know on earth today.

This ideology is meant to help create a spark that will help grow each society into a stronger economy that safeguards the environment and earth. It might even create a super boom for its economy with the right balance to sustain all life and resources. This requires that each region of the world make the most efficient and most affordable products or services that meet people's wants and needs without hurting the environment and at the same time healing earth. If we all do our share around the world, we will learn a new way of living life in balance and harmony with earth. Earth and mankind can live together in "Universal Balance in Harmony" in peace and prosperity forever!

Conclusion

The first step in this great change will set the stage for this ideology to reverse the damage already done by past generations. We must all come to a consensus and admit our wrongs in our regions, and we all must pitch in to get this fixed ASAP so earth can provide us forever with the fruits we so much enjoy!

Al Gore has brought awareness in his Nobel Peace Prize lecture in 2007 entitled "Our Purpose." This is just the tip of the iceberg, and we need further understanding of earth's current condition and whether our actions today will harm the earth now and into the future. Every nation should do its own diligence to figure out what is best for their country, but at the same time have an open mind to everyone else around the world as to where you fit in. The United Nations should be a counselor to every nation around the world to give them guidance to help all of us to solve and create solutions that will quickly cure the ills done to. We must do these things without thinking about cost, but instead we should think about how we can all live in harmony with earth today and forever! God bless mankind, Mother Earth, and our Universe to live in balance and in harmony forever more! Godspeed to all things God created! Peace and love be with you all!

As the United States government or any government starts to sell its new inventions and services business ventures, the revenue from the sale of the products and services should also begin immediately to bring down national debt. Then, governments can slowly reverse taxation at a slow rate and eventually eliminate them someday, as the new government businesses begin to develop and grow.

The foremost priority is to pay off national debts owed to other countries or persons around the world to keep the peace we all live now. The second priority is to eliminate taxation for good. The third priority is to build every country into a surplus country, to be prepared for unexpected incidents that only God knows.

Those are the main goals for the economy of any nation. Also, note we're not forgetting the main reason why this is being done to a nation's economy: the earth must be respected and always be the main priority for mankind to exist. It is home to all of us. God speed to all nations to get on track with *Universal Balance in Harmony*.

This injection system theory should create balance for a nation to prosper and preserve its natural resources more efficiently—saving and repairing the environment, healing earth as quickly as possible to get us on track at 100% balance in harmony. It will give each country a broader understanding of its place in the world. We need to be more aware with sounder judgment and wiser with a better understanding of our surroundings. At the same, we should be keeping an open mind on all things and using more caution in all new developed enterprise regarding how and what we do to affect us now and into the future.

Sharing and working together every country with *Universal Balance in Harmony* will help keep the world market economies and earth's finite resources on track. This theory brings out the best in mankind working together. It sheds more transparency upon the world. This will help speed up healing ourselves and the economy and keep earth from going dark. We all must use earth's bounty wisely so we can enjoy it now and for the future generations to come.

I repeat again: we will always put Mother Earth first

ahead of our own wants and needs. If, our wants and needs are too great for Mother Earth to continue to produce a safe haven for both mankind and earth, we have to look for other alternatives.

One thing we can do is to seek natural resources out in the universe and to colonize other planets, especially if the population grows too fast for Mother Earth to sustain. This is a challenge is to all mankind: To seek and find while making our life's priority existence with the "Universal Balance and Harmony Theory." It is the vital key to life and for the world to coexist in balance forever! God bless the Universe, our home— earth, mankind, and to my own nation, the USA.

Author

Steven Rhei Pena

This theory I bring forth to the world didn't come to me overnight. It took a lifetime of studying and being challenged in lifelong experiences as well in college. It's a theory on how to improve our living standards as well as our surroundings in our world. I thought long and hard all my life while always having an open mind, with a different mindset and comparison in thinking.

I bring compassion to all things bad or good, intellectual thinking as to the whys, and an open concept to broader understanding of all things good and bad. I observe with a critical, intelligent mindset why things are this way now, how they used to be, and how they can be better in the future. I have a systematic way of thinking in a logical way to determine when something happens whether it is bad or good. These were the methods I process and ponder in my mind over and over again in order to bring something fair for everything living and not living on earth from the past to now and into the future!

As a person from a middle class family, I kept an open

mind and tried to understand the conditions around us, whether good or bad, and seeking answers from whys. Why do we do things the way we do? Why? Is it good or is it bad when we do these things we do? Do these things help earth or the poor, middle-class, rich, or everybody and everything? Does what we do benefit mankind for the present or for the future? Does it only help just one class of people to enjoy a higher standard of living or does it help everyone? Does it benefit animal and plant life and safeguard earth's finite natural resources or does it exhaust resources for mankind's uses? Has anyone other than scientists known the true mathematical equation of mankind's numbers to live and sustain a safe, peaceful, abundant living mode in co-existence now and into the future with the resources from Mother Earth? Is what we do now good or bad for Mother Earth or vice versa?

My mind not only wonders about our way of life for all humanity, but I also wonder whether God will be happy with the conditions between humanity and earth today, tomorrow, and beyond. Will God be happy if we proceed this way in life? Will what we do today cause regret in the future? Will things stay the same or change for the better or worse?

I felt as if at times, I'm both the Thinker and the Watcher in one. I try to understand why things are the way they are, as well as to witness what has happened, what could happen in the future if things evolve for the better or worse for all things created on earth, and what I've seen repeated when these situations arise time and time again with the same outcome everywhere.

I even question my own thoughts: Is this the right way to think? Will everyone want this to be so, and will God above be proud of the outcome whatever mankind does or does not do? Will mankind like it or dislike it? Can I make everyone on earth happy? Never an easy solution to ponder!

I do not think I'm better than anyone else, just a man who cares deeply for all things living and not living in this universe. I learned to love it all, the good and the bad. I prefer the good, but without the bad I wouldn't appreciate the good so well. I love all life and wish we could coexist forever in our physical, healthy forms, living in harmony, growing the best part in ourselves and refine it over and over—making it wiser, happier, stronger, more intelligent, more peaceful in content, more of everything that is good and better for ourselves!

Living in such a way will make us feel better connected to ourselves and the universe and as close to heaven as man's soul can get without actually being in heaven! With all due respect, we must do this without hurting earth to a point of destruction.

This theory has been on my mind for a long time. I originally wrote this theory in 1996, but it lacked something. Then after I graduated from the University of Texas at San Antonio in December 2012, the full spectrum came to me. I completed my Bachelors of Arts degree with a major in Political Science and two minors: International Studies and Business Administration.

Life for me has been very hard—it's a story in a story to be told one day. But the best part of my life now will be getting this book published. It's been a great burden in my mind for me to think that if I die, this ideology or theory will die with me and will never be exposed to the minds of mankind!

If you are reading this, I must have completed this, and that is awesome to know! Finally, relief! I feel the universe is off my back! I say this because I know and believe 100% that this idea came from God. This book is a new guide for all to keep mankind and earth moving forward into the future with God's love for mankind, in balance and peace.

It's the best feeling for mankind to know that all God has created—mankind, earth, the cosmos, and everything—is safe! In my opinion, God will feel more excited and happier to know what He created—mankind, earth, and the universe—are co-existing together more peacefully in balance for all things. While this theory will help mankind keep evolving into the future with higher heights of living on earth and learning to safeguard Mother Earth, the cosmos and beyond will be our final exploration for resources and growth to bring balance to our civilization and world. Someday when we colonize the universe, we must bring the same principles from earth and safeguard the new worlds in our universe and onto other galaxies! Mankind and everything on earth are here to live in "Universal Balance and Harmony" forever more! Peace!